THE HANNIBAL SQUARE HERITAGE COLLECTION

PHOTOGRAPHS AND ORAL HISTORIES

Winter Park | Florida | USA
Foreword | Kristin Congdon
Peter Schreyer | Project
Director and Photo Editor

The Hannibal Square Heritage Collection
Photographs and Oral Histories

ISBN: 978-1-886104-86-0

The Florida Historical Society Press
435 Brevard Avenue
Cocoa, FL 32922
http://myfloridahistory.org/fhspress

The Hannibal Square Heritage Center is located at 642 West New England Avenue in Winter Park | Florida.

For more information please call 407-539-2680 or check out their website at www.hannibalsquareheritagecenter.org.

Book design: www.scholldesign.com

Heritage Collection Team:
Fairolyn Livingston | Community Native and Project Chief Historian
Mary Daniels | Community Native and Historian
Kim Mould | Historian
Ronald Habin, Ph.D. | Anthropologist
Phyllis Moore | Community Liaison
Bonnie Swain | Community Liaison
Peter Schreyer | Project Director and Photo Editor

Everyday people living in the Hannibal Square neighborhood of Winter Park, Florida took most the photographs in this book. They were reproduced from small snapshots taken with inexpensive amateur cameras. Professionals with better cameras shot the sharper photographs in this publication.

In the images, residents got married and had children. They purchased cars and motorcycles. They sat on Santa's knee, danced, had homecoming parades, played sports, and dreamed about bright futures. They held jobs as soldiers, chefs, ministers, seamstresses, and teachers. They dressed up and dressed down, traveled to Washington D.C., and mixed with accomplished people like the Boyer Brothers and Paul Robeson. They found joy in living and suffered hardships.

In these photographs, we see the way the neighborhood used to be, mostly during the mid-twentieth century. It had dirt roads. One home was swallowed by a sinkhole. Community gathering spaces included the Ideal Women's Club, Moore's Tea Room, Ben Miles Soda Shop, Hannibal Square Elementary School, and the Ruby M. Ball Annex at the Winter Park Community Center. Looking through these pages we witness segregation and the presence of the NAACP and the Human Relations Council. In short, we observe history through the eyes of one small African American community.

The Hannibal Square community was established in the late 1880s on the west side of Winter Park, on the other side of the railroad tracks from affluent white people's houses. As anthropologist Dr. Ronald Habin claims, this section of the town developed "as a residential section for the 'colored' help." He further makes it clear that the Hannibal Square residents, like blacks in so many other southern towns, "endured the hardships of civic de-annexation, re-annexation, and the ugly ramifications codified by racially segregated Jim Crow laws." African Americans could not cross the railroad tracks to the white sections after dark. And as Habin reports, failure to comply with these laws could result in beatings or even death.

Regardless of the hatred and violence around them, people living in Hannibal Square strived to make their lives meaningful and rich in ways that resonate with all United States citizens. Their snapshots bear witness to the character of the residents and the strength of the neighborhood.

Everyday photographs were not taken with artistic intentions; instead, they were meant to be documentary. Sometimes, however, they function both as documents and aesthetic objects. The famed critic Susan Sontag recognized that the "unassuming functional snapshot may be as visually interesting as the most acclaimed fine art photography." Snapshots, such as the ones in this book, may be oddly composed or humorously telling. They can place us back into their historical context, and like good art, they can teach us something new about ourselves and the ways in which we understand the world. The images in this book that span the twentieth century, in their honest and unintentional manner, reveal the spirit of Winter Park's Hannibal Square neighborhood, as well as celebratory moments. There are insights in the gestures, glances, and relationships of the subjects to their surroundings. But beyond that, looking at them from our present time and place, they aesthetically communicate universal truths about the relevance of family ties and community spaces. They also, often inadvertently, tell a story about race relations in the twentieth century. When we as viewers engage with the photographs and descriptive voices in the essays, we better understand the present world in which we live. These documents, along with numerous others that provide the foundation for the Hannibal Square Heritage Center, inform the public, both inside and outside the Winter Park community. Today, there are many collectors who have an interest in everyday snapshots and photographs, and museums are beginning to follow their lead.

Hannibal Square Heritage Center | Winter Park FL.

The Heritage Collection: Photographs and Oral History of West Winter Park, was started in the 1990s as the African American neighborhood was becoming gentrified and local businesses and traditional meeting spaces were demolished and replaced with upscaled businesses. As the gentrification took place, real estate prices rose and community gathering spaces for African Americans gave way to expensive shopping areas. As community historian Fairolyn Livingston remarked, the people in her community became "strangers in their own land."

Under the direction of Peter Schreyer, executive director of Crealdé School of Art in Winter Park, the documentary project took root. Peter had been photographing the Hannibal Square neighborhood for years, and like the residents of the area, he mourned the destruction of the traditional community. The idea to form the Heritage Collection came from a conference Peter attended in California, where the Los Angeles County Library made a presentation on their successful documentation projects that took place in diverse areas of Los Angeles. When Peter returned to Florida, he told Ronnie Moore, then the Director of the Winter Park Community Center, about it. Together, they decided to build an archive on west Winter Park.

In order to record and celebrate the disappearing community life, in 2001, Peter, Ronnie, and other community members encouraged Hannibal Square residents to contribute family snapshots from their private collections to help establish a permanent archive. Individuals brought in shoeboxes and envelopes filled with photographs. Two men from Tallahassee drove to Winter Park with a cooler, filled with framed photographs they took off their walls. Valued family photographs were professionally copied and quickly returned to their lenders. The documentary team, Fairolyn Livingston, Ron Habin, Kim Mould, and Peter Schreyer and field assistants Phyllis Moore and Bonnie Swain, received enthusiastic support from the community. A rich documented history of the Hannibal Square community was soon realized. Before long, talks began on where to permanently house the materials.

A partnership between the residents of west Winter Park, Crealdé School of Art, and the City of Winter Park was formed to construct a building. In 2007, after three years of planning, The Hannibal Square Heritage Center was built with a grant from the city's Community Redevelopment Agency, which helps sustain its work. According to Peter Schreyer, "it took on a life of its own," and by all accounts, the Hannibal Square Heritage Center is a grand achievement. It is now viewed as a model for community art centers around the country. Resident ownership of their recorded and exhibited history is a key to its success.

Interest in the ways in which people document their own lives through photographic means is growing around the world. When the images in this book were taken, the photographers thought that their work would be of value to only a small group of people. But this collection of Hannibal Square photographs not only represents a specific group of people during a particular time and place; it also gives us insight to the human condition. We all crave connections to those around us; we celebrate successes and rites of passage; and we strive to become better people. This is the story of the Hannibal Square neighborhood, but in some ways, it is a story that belongs to all of us. These photographs teach us fundamental truths about what it means to be human. They reflect on how we all structure our lives and find pleasure in everyday moments. These photographs, in their sometimes quirky, unpolished manner, communicate that the best times are often those where we see ourselves in the places and spaces where we most readily belong. **kristin congdon** | Ph.D. Professor *Emerita*, university of central Florida

references: Foster, John. "Photography, Vernacular."
In The New Encyclopedia of Southern Culture.
Volume 23: Folk Art, edited by Carol Crown and Cheryl Rivers,
146-149. Chapel Hill: University of North Carolina Press, 2013.
Sontag, Susan. On Photography. New York: Penguin Classics, 2008.
Kristin Congdon, Ph.D. Professor Emerita, University of Central
Florida, Member of the Heritage Center Advisory Committee.

This photograph was taken in front of my family's business which originally started out as "Baby's Lunchbox." The business was named after the lady who is sitting there, my grandmother, Lessie Mae Marsh, who was nicknamed "Baby Young." The photograph was taken in about 1956, and it shows my oldest brother, Eric Knight, when he was about three years old. The police officer that is standing there is a well-respected police officer, Mr. Fields, one of the first black police officers in the Winter Park community. You can see how elated my brother is to see Mr. Fields. He was always a person who patrolled and walked the area making sure that everything on the Westside was in order.

We need to communicate to our young that this is where we are from and the only way it will stay ours is if they become part of it now. We have got to raise our youths to understand exactly what their heritage is and get them to embrace that now. My family business has been here for four generations, over seventy years, and I am committed to bringing more black business to the Westside.

Mr. Robert Knight
West Winter Park Business Owner
August 24 | 2002

This is on Welbourne Avenue in the 1960s. We will call it "Children at Play." These are my daughters, Bonnie and Donna, and their community playmate. The little girl in the middle is Bonnie Swain, and the taller of the children is Donna. They are on Welbourne where the streets were paved at that time. Most of the streets were sand streets, but Welbourne had been paved. This is looking down Welbourne towards Park Avenue. It is probably from the corner of Virginia and looking toward New York and on towards Central Park.

Joyce Swain and Carol Anderson
Sisters and Lifelong West Winter Park Residents
November 8 | 2002

This photograph has lots of memories to anybody on the Westside. This is a picture of the Boyer Brothers, probably taken in the 1950s. They were a nationally known duet of gospel singers. They were really hometown boys from Winter Park. This is Horace and this is James. Now, they were friends of ours from elementary school through high school. They went all over the United States singing, playing, and connecting with other renown groups.

This photograph was taken at a local radio station in Orlando, WHOO, during one of their broadcasts. The Boyer Brothers were brilliant people and very accomplished. James is now a minister in the Kansas area. Horace is also very well known. He was at the Smithsonian Institution, and he has done work at Elmhurst College in Massachusetts in the area of music. Horace is an outstanding historian of African American Music, and he often comes here on a consultant basis. He has been at Rollins for the Black History Observance several times, and he comes to the Zora Neale Hurston Festival as a facilitator, because he has written several volumes of African American music. What Carol has not shared with you yet is that when they had concerts here at home she too appeared on their programs as a singer! Oh Joyce, I just appeared as a soloist. These people were really gospel singers. I had a deep appreciation for that, but couldn't sing that kind of music. It takes a certain kind of person, a certain kind of voice and makeup, to sing it as well as the Boyer Brothers did.

carol anderson and joyce swain
sisters and lifelong west winter park residents
november 8 | 2002

To Mommy Evelyn & ~
The Boyer Brothe~
"Best Wishes"

This is the beautiful Carol Walker Everett at her kindergarten graduation in 1957 with her diploma in her hand. Isn't she cute? The ceremony was held at Bethel Baptist Church. All of the graduating students took individual and group photos after the ceremony.

Mrs. Carol Walker Everett
Teacher, Dr. Phillips High School
Lifelong Resident West Winter Park
February 16 | 2002

This is my cousin, Christine Dixon on the left, along with one of her friends, Melenese Jordan. They had gone to the annual fair, the Central Florida Fair, and as was the custom or thing that everyone did, they had their picture taken. The fair during that time was located downtown Orlando on Livingston Street. The fairground is now located on West Colonial Drive. I'm not really sure what year this was taken, but it had to be in the early 1960s before they graduated high school.

Mrs. carol walker everett
teacher, Dr. phillips High school
Lifelong Resident west winter park
February 16 | 2002

This photograph is of my grandmother, Lessie Mae Marsh, and her first cousin, Willie Lee, at the Duck Inn in West Winter Park, later known as the Sportz Inn. This photograph was taken in the 1960s and represents the transition of the business from a kitchen to a bar and kitchen. The Duck Inn was a little blues juke joint, and everyone would come and dance out on the open porch in front of the bar. Mr. Robert Knight

West Winter Park Business Owner

December 3 | 2003

That's my cousin, Eddie Terrell Jr., at the Welbourne Nursery and Kindergarten, one of the oldest institutions in the community for kids. The Day Nursery has been there…my brother is 62, maybe, and he attended school there. This photograph was taken in the late 1960s, maybe. Eddie today would be in his thirties. They had a fair at the nursery, and he was all dressed up as a cowboy that day. Eddie was approximately two or three years old. **mrs. Hazel walker**
lifelong west winter park resident
february 16 | 2002

This is Eva Straughter in the 1950s with her Chevrolet. Eva's family was one of the founding families of the City of Winter Park. She's standing out in front of her 1956 or 1957 Chevrolet. She is just standing there admiring her car. She was standing behind her car and someone just took a photo of Eva Straughter. Her house is located on the corner of Lyman and New York Avenues by the railroad tracks.

MRS. CAROL WALKER EVERETT
Teacher, Dr. Phillips High School
Lifelong Resident West Winter Park
February 16 | 2002

A love of cars runs in the family. I have my dad, Robert R. Hall's car, a 1968 Chevy. I still drive it, in fact I drove it today. My brother has three kids, and they know to hang on to this car, because it is part of the family heritage. My family came to Winter Park from Georgia in 1924. This is a photograph of just the brothers, Clyde, Willis, and me, and it was taken in 1938 in front of our home and in front of a 1935 Chevrolet. In 1939, we drove this particular car to the World's Fair in New York. The trip took several days, but we had relatives in North Carolina and in New Jersey. The thing I remember most about the World's Fair is that I had never seen pizza before!

This was taken at 790 Swoope Avenue, but the address is now 796 Swoope, and the house is still standing. You know, my brother and I used to sit over on Park Avenue and count cars. One afternoon, we counted six. Six! And there were very few people. Everybody knew everybody. And they knew where you were supposed to be!

Mr. Richard Robert Hall, Jr.
Retired chief Master sergeant
United States Air Force
February 16 | 2002

We believe this was taken in the 1950s in one of the department stores in downtown Orlando, either Kress, Grants, or Woolworths. I am inclined to believe it was Kress. This little boy is our brother who was about five or six. His name is Jesse, and he was named for our grandmother, Jessie Latimer.

He was her favorite of all of us, probably because he was named for her! At Christmas, we had celebrations in our churches, in our homes, and we always had Christmas dances at the Community Center or at the Ideal Woman's Club. These were sometimes formal, dress up occasions, depending on who gave them. Our community was a close knit community, so when you had a party it wasn't like it is now where people just bombard you or come and cause all sorts of problems. The parents were very strict about who could come and how long they could stay. We don't have any photographs of the parties. Picture taking was not something we thought about. We just wanted to dance and have a good time!

carol Anderson and Joyce swain
sisters and Lifelong west
winter park Residents
November 8 | 2002

Joyce might know more about this photograph than I do. I know that the wedding was in the home of Robert Gibson here in Winter Park on Seminole Drive. My mother was the housekeeper and Mr. Fortson was the butler. Of course, after the wedding ceremony they had a reception, and they both served. I don't have any memory of their names or who they were. Sally…I think I remember that her first name was Sally. At that time, a lot of our people also got married at home. The Ideal Woman's Club was, in our community at that time, the place to have any kind of reception. The old wooden building was quite the thing in its day. You could decorate it and dress it up for parties and receptions. We were quite proud of that building. Couples often were married in their churches and still had their receptions there because a lot of the churches didn't have separate halls. Yes, that building got a lot of use. It was a community building. It was the meeting place in the neighborhood.

carol anderson and joyce swain sisters
lifelong west winter park residents
november 8 | 2002

This is a photograph of Justine Langwood, my best friend, at Mobile Beach, Altamonte Springs, Florida, in the early 1950s. We had no other beach to go to. This is where we black folks could go to the beach. On a typical Sunday morning, we would have gone to church, changed clothes, and go. We could always get a ride, because we were pretty young girls. We never really had the chance to do and be what we probably would have liked to have done. But you know how it was with blacks. We were just held down. Nothing you could do about it. Mrs. Julia Cleveland
Longtime West Winter Park Resident
February 16 | 2002

This is Missouri Ambrose, and it was in Charlie and Missouri Ambrose's home that the Mt. Moriah Missionary Baptist Church was organized. This must have been around 1900, because the church celebrated one hundred years in 2000. It was the establishment of the first Baptist religion church in Winter Park. Missouri was my dad's grandmother. His name was Theodore Moore, and she was his grandmother. Her daughter was my grandmother, Ozella Moore. Missouri and Charlie were the parents of quite a large family. There were about seven daughters and three sons. She probably had a position in the church similar to that of a deaconess, taking care of things for communion, taking care of the linen, making baptismal gowns, and serving in the youth ministry. The shawl and the long dress…this is definitely an outfit for going to church, wouldn't you say, Carol? Joyce swain and carol Anderson
sisters and Lifelong west winter Park Residents
November 8 | 2002

Moore Paints sponsored this softball team in the 1960s. The members included, from the left, Winston Grey, Ernest "Skinny" Daniels, David Whitaker, and fourth from the left, Attorney Warren Williams. The team was on their way to Washington, D.C. for the National Softball Tournament. MRS. Mary Daniels
Longtime west winter Park Resident
February 16 | 2002

This is a picture of my aunt, Pearl T. Reed, who was the Principal of Hannibal Elementary School, which was located in Winter Park on two streets, Pennsylvania and New England. This photo was actually taken in the building that was on Pennsylvania facing Ward Chapel. It was taken around 1964. My aunt was very strict. She had very high values, high morals, and the same high morals she had she looked to others to do the same thing. She had one daughter by marriage, Lillian. Actually, the entire community called her "Ma Pearl," so the whole community thought of her as mother. My aunt always worked in the teaching profession. She died in 1979 and is buried at Pineywoods Cemetery.

Mrs. Pearl Ings
Longtime West Winter Park Resident
and Property Owner
August 24 | 2002

This is Samuel "Sammie" Charles Perry. Samuel Charles Perry was a graduate of Hungerford High School, and he was the Drum Major in 1958. That's when they had only one Drum Major, rather than several as they continued on in future years. Under his leadership, he successfully led the band to district and state band competitions. He earned a basketball scholarship to Kentucky State University; however by the time he left to go, the war picked him up. When he came back from the military, where he was honorably discharged after serving in Vietnam, he was never the same. Vietnam took care of him mentally, and he knew that was what it was. He always kept a poster on his refrigerator that stuck out in all our minds: OF ALL THE THINGS THAT I HAVE LOST IT IS MY MIND I MISS MOST. That was so true for Samuel Charles because he was a very sharp student, an excellent student in high school. Over the years, Samuel Charles became a hermit and eventually just died of loneliness in his house, by himself.

Mrs. carol walker Everett
Teacher, Dr. Phillips High School
Lifelong Resident of west winter Park
February 16 | 2002

One beautiful morning a group of lovely ladies were invited to my home to share an occasion to give honor to an ill friend of Mrs. Anne Belle Woodard, Mrs. Josephine Gary. Mrs. Gary, one of the elderly citizens of Winter Park who was beloved by all that knew her, was hospitalized and diagnosed with many physical problems. Mrs. Woodard called Mrs. Gary's neighbor, Mrs. Louise Charlton, who then called me knowing I was a Licensed Practical Nurse and Mrs. Gary needed home care. I did not personally know Mrs. Gary or Mrs. Woodard, but I was indeed interested in helping. It was one of the most rewarding experiences in my life to see friends working together to help a friend in need. I was there every morning to give Mrs. Gary her shots and medications. Observing the relationship between the friends, there was something in their character that I admired and wanted to add to my own life: the spirit in action of love and friendship. On September 16, 1980, the same group of ladies that attended the luncheon got together and organized a club in honor of Mrs. Woodard, who suggested the name "Key." Mrs. Charlton added "Chain," thus we became "The Key Chain Club," one in spirit of love and friendship. The key is a symbol of friendship, the cross, anchor, and heart symbols extend from the key and stand for Faith, Hope, and Charity.

Mrs. Vera Lee
Retired Licensed Practical Nurse
February 16 | 2002

This is a photograph of Mr. Walter Green taken on Church Street in approximately 1963. On the weekend, people would go to Church Street in Orlando to have pictures made. It was a better quality than what you could get at home. So we would make a special trip to Church Street for a good picture. Each photo would cost about $3.00.

Mrs. Martha Bryant Hall
wife of Longtime Winter Park Resident
Rev. Jerry Hall, Pastor
Prayer Mission Church of God in Christ
February 16 | 2002

This was at the Welbourne Day Nursery. I am in this picture sitting in front on the left hand side next to the little boy. The children had been told to look straight ahead. Only one student didn't follow directions... The woman in the nurse's uniform is Minnie May Ball.

Linda Walker
Life Long Winter Park Resident
January 17 | 2005

I found this in my photograph album, but it is actually my step-mother, Siraella Moore's photograph. In the 1940s, she was the owner of Moore's Tea Room located in the 500 block of New England Avenue. I don't know exactly where or when this photograph was taken, but I do know that the little boy in the picture is Wesley Moore. I don't know the names of any of the individuals in the photograph. It appears as though the men were soldiers possibly stationed at the local military base in the 1940s. I have heard that the Ideal Woman's Club on Pennsylvania Avenue often invited young military men to social events held at the old Ideal Woman's Club.

Mrs. Phylis Moore
Lifelong West Winter Park Resident
Heritage Collection Project Team Member
December 9 | 2002

This photograph was taken on December 22, 1959 on our wedding day! The bride is me, Annie Smith Burns, and the groom is my husband, Joe Burns. My maid of honor is Barbara Woodard, and the best man is Harold Merrell and the pastor is Rev. B.J. Lane, my pastor at the time. We got married in my mother and father Willie and Ben Smith's home at 431 West Morse Boulevard. At the little ceremony it was just my family and my husband's family. We had our reception at the Ideal Woman's Club and we invited several guests to that event. Our reception was held in the old Ideal Woman's Club building, which is no longer standing.

Mrs. Annie Burns
Mr. Joe Burns
Longtime Winter Park Residents
August 16, 2003

This is my grandfather, Mr. Dempsey Phillips. He was born in Richmond, Virginia, and he was a chef on the train. He married Matilda and they resided in Valdosta, Georgia. To that family, Laura and Lena were born. Dempsey settled with his family on eighteen acres in Winter Park, Florida, where he farmed. He also had cows and hogs. He was a chef at the old Seminole Hotel and every Thanksgiving, he held a family gathering. Dempsey Phillips died Tuesday, June 7, 1932. Mrs. Rose Bynum

Lifelong West Winter Park Resident

September 9 | 2003

Mrs. Evelyn Sea Perkins is a native Floridian. She was born in Palatka, Florida in 1917, and she came to Winter Park in 1942 with her six children. Mrs. Perkins, a seamstress and cook by trade, owned and operated a barbecue takeout in Hannibal Square in the early 1960s. This photograph was taken in 1947 and she is wearing a dress that is one of her creations. Mrs. Perkins is my grandmother. She is 86 years old and still resides in Winter Park!

Mrs. Dionne Mikell
Longtime Winter Park Resident
August 20 | 2003

This was during the time, I believe, it was the 1960s. My first cousin Francis Wilson is holding her first born, nicknamed "Peanut," in front of our house at 851 Canton Avenue. As you can see, she is standing in front of my brother Jake's 1959 Pontiac. We called him Jake, but his name is Isaiah Bailey. At that time, we had dirt streets.

MRS. Pandora Carter Taylor
Lifelong Winter Park Resident
November 15 | 2003

This is also on the Carter property at 841 Canton Avenue, Winter Park in the 1960s. This is my oldest brother Jake's first motorcycle. So the neighborhood kids are just sitting on it, taking a picture, because it was always kids on the property. So the kids were like our sisters and brothers because my mother and father fed every one of them they could. Mrs. pandora carter Taylor
Lifelong winter Park Resident
November 15 | 2003

Miss Homecoming

Rose Charlton Bynum

Attendants

Mae Frances Williams

Vivian Pleasants

We could not attend Winter Park High School because of segregation. So we had a choice of either Hungerford High or Jones High, and I chose Hungerford High School. This is a photograph of the Homecoming Parade in 1948, with me as Miss Homecoming for Hungerford High. I am in the middle and my attendants are Mae Francis Williams and Vivian Pleasants. The Homecoming Parade would start in Eatonville and continue down Park Avenue in Winter Park. Miss Homecoming and her attendants were chosen by popular vote. Hungerford had a good football team and the football games and Homecoming were big events!   Mrs. Rose Bynum
Lifelong West Winter Park Resident
September 9 | 2003

This is my sister Arizola at about 15 years old wearing a skirt that she made. The girls used to dance together and one of their favorites at the time was the square dance. I am the girl in the straw hat and shorts. We had to share the backyard with the chickens and ducks.

Lurline Daniels Fletcher
Longtime Winter Park Resident
January 17 | 2005

This is Mr. Herbert and Alma Roberts in Ruby Ball's front yard at 773 New England Avenue. In the 1950s, they were "socialites of their time." There was a "Who's Who" list in the community and the Roberts' were on that list. In his later years, Mr. Roberts was the chef at the former Mark II Dinner Theatre.

Linda walker
Life Long winter Park Resident
January 17 | 2005

Mr. Herbert Roberts holding his daughter Sharon in their backyard on Denning Avenue. In the early 1980s the property was swallowed by a sinkhole. Notice neighborhood outhouses and chicken coops in the background for another look and feel of west Winter Park in the late 1950s.

Linda Walker
Life Long Winter Park Resident
January 17 | 2005

This is Usher Board #1 on the grounds of Mt. Moriah Missionary Baptist Church at the corner of Pennsylvania and Lyman Avenues, in the late '50s early '60s. The building in the background is Ben Miles Soda Shop. The Miles family lived on the 2nd floor. The people in the picture left to right; Gennie V. Golden, Lula Durant, Sarah Perry, Margaret Haynie, and Hattie Shumate. These women were the doorkeepers of the church. They seated worshipers, helped take the offering, and ran errands for the membership while service was going on. And holding out a fan when children were chewing gum.

Juanita Rountree
Life Long Winter Park Resident
January 17 | 2005

This is our second grade class at Hannibal Square Elementary School in 1952. Mrs. Edith Sykes was our teacher, I can name most of them:
If I can remember, this was one of two second grade classes. I guess they called us the first generation of the war babies. Following this class they had to consider building Webster Elementary because the classes were getting larger and larger. Mrs. Sykes lived a couple of houses from where we lived, and had to be

Mr. Edward Anderson
Lifelong Winter Park Resident
August 16 | 2003

Hannibal Square Elementary School
second grade class

First row, left to Right: Mary Hector | Gwen Banks | Altamese Mitchell | Adrena Jordan | Joe Ann Jordan | Libby Bryant | Edith Boyer | Brenda McKinney | Carolyn Johnson | Gloria Simmons | Dianne Perry.

Second row: Ronald Jones | Clarence Griffin | Adolphus Jones | Willie Cooper | Leotis Anderson | Willie Bolden | Willie Jordan (?) | Sam Brown | James Singleton | Cornelius Harris.

Third row: Unable to identify | Joe Hill | Robert Philpott | Bertell Delancy | George Tooley | Edward Anderson | John Jacobs | Isaiah Stanley | Isaiah "Jake" Bailey | Jimmy Smith.

on our best behavior at school. The teachers lived in the neighborhood, and they knew your parents. They went to the same churches. It was actually a neighborhood school at that time. We have had a couple of reunions, the last one was we had was a couple of years ago, and we had it right here in this building (Community Center). I see a few of my classmates on a regular basis, Willie Cooper, George Tooley, and Jake.

Welcome to Easter Sunday 1958 with the prominent Ball family. This formal portrait was taken by E.B. Mitchell, a Black locally renowned Orlando photographer. Featured on this special day are children Loretta and Lawrence and parents Hayward Wesley Ball and Ruby M. Ball. As locals know, the Ruby M. Ball Annex at the Winter Park Community Center was named in honor of Ms. Ball, who for years taught at Hungerford High School. Her dedication to local children was legendary. For example, if they were having problems keeping their grades up, she would tutor them in her home.

Ms. Ruby M. Ball served as President of the local chapter of the NAACP. At the time of her passing, she was President of the Human Relations Council. This fine organization was created to diminish racial hostility and resolve community differences. Many people considered the Human Relations Council the true voice of the community.

Loretta Ball
Life-Long west winter Park Resident
september 22 | 2007

Ms. Ella Mae Redfin was a Hannibal Square community fixture from 1942 into the 1980s. You'd be hard pressed to find anyone who loved the people of the square more than Ms. Ella Mae.

She would be down at Moore's Tea Room, talking to people at the barber shop and learning about and adding to the neighborhood's excitement at any time of day or night.

In this photograph from the late 1960s, she poses – not with her own bike as she never rode, but she typically posed behind one or (perhaps not coincidently) in front of a Cadillac. Across the street and over her shoulder, see a rooming house owned by Mr. Wes Glen.

Fairolyn Livingston
Long-time west winter park resident
Local Historian
september 22 | 2007

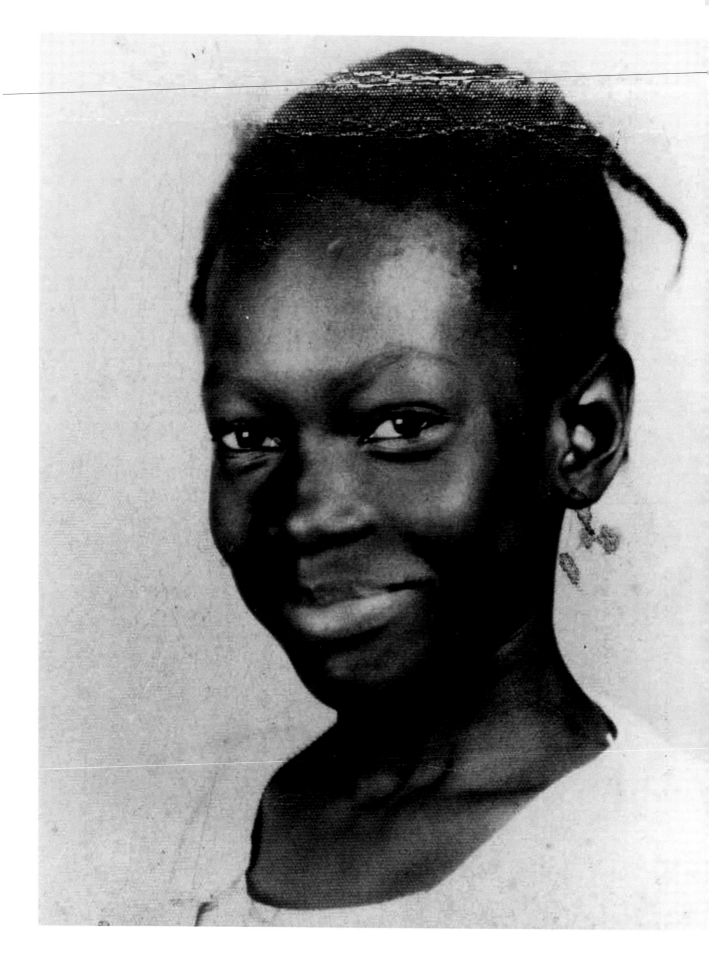

This is my 1957-1958, 6th grade picture at Hannibal Square Elementary, a segregated school which according to Brown v. Board of Education was separate and unequal. However that never stopped us from academic and social success. Our teachers challenged and lovingly admonished us to rise above the stereotypical characteristics of Blacks from white society that didn't expect black people to succeed due to a lack of intelligence and drive. My hair was short on the sides and long up top, so I always wore a large plait up top. I look happy because I loved school. Growing up in the 1940s and 50s, dark skin, large nose and lips were not desired traits so I never felt beautiful. It wasn't until the 1960s and James Brown's "I'm Black and I'm Proud," that I being to look at myself differently.

Fairolyn Livingston
Long-Time West Winter Park Resident
Local Historian
september 22 | 2007

This picture was taken on Easter Sunday 1940s. Featured in this photograph are (from left) Jackie Ball, her godsister Sharon Roberts, Cynthia Ball, and friend Olivia. The building directly behind the girls is the community recreation center. The smaller building on the far left housed the old Hannibal Square Elementary School Principal's Office and a few classrooms. The following year young Jackie developed rheumatic fever and died of complications from rheumatoid arthritis.

Loretta Ball
Life-Long west winter park resident
september 22 | 2007

This is a picture of Juanita Rountree in the early 1960s at age 11 or 12, standing in the middle of Comstock Avenue before the streets were paved.

Juanita Rountree
Life-Long Winter Park Resident
september 22 | 2007

This preservation of Landonia Estelle Lemon Frazier was photographed in the early 1900s. Ms. Frazier is the daughter of Will Frazier, one of the founding fathers of Winter Park. Will came from Virginia and he was the son of the master of the plantation where his mother was a slave. Will was always free and when he became a teenager, his father allowed him to leave and he came to Florida to work because they were getting ready to put railroads and streets in the Winter Park area. Will Frazier was a very fair man with straight hair who looked more like a white man than a black man. On occasions when people would see him and his wife together they assumed that she was his maid or servant.

Will died in a train incident in Winter Park. Some said he was pushed into the path of an oncoming train. Will's granddaughter, Wilhelmina Allen, described him as a very nice man. Members of his wife's family were pioneers of Ward Chapel AME Church and actually paid a good portion of the money to build the first church building.

cecil and Rita Allen
Long-Time west winter park Residents
september 22 | 2007

These, indeed, are the "men of Mount Moriah" church. Pictured here just after services in the early 1950s are the deacons, officers, movers and shakers of this significant community institution. Interestingly, many of these gentlemen owned their own businesses and worked for the wealthy of east Winter Park. Some owned residential and commercial rental property, one owned a sundry shop, another headed a firm that renovated old homes, and several owned local rooming houses. They were simultaneously employed as chauffeurs, house servants, and gardeners.

Juanita Rountree
Life-Long Winter Park Resident
september 22 | 2007

This is a picture of Willie Lee Snow taken December 1959. We might say that this is the very essence of teen talk, 1950s style. Notice the rotary dial phone, recessed phone stand, and stool. Willie is dressed in the latest 1959 fashions and is probably headed out for fun. Margaret Perkins
Long-time west winter park resident
september 22 | 2007

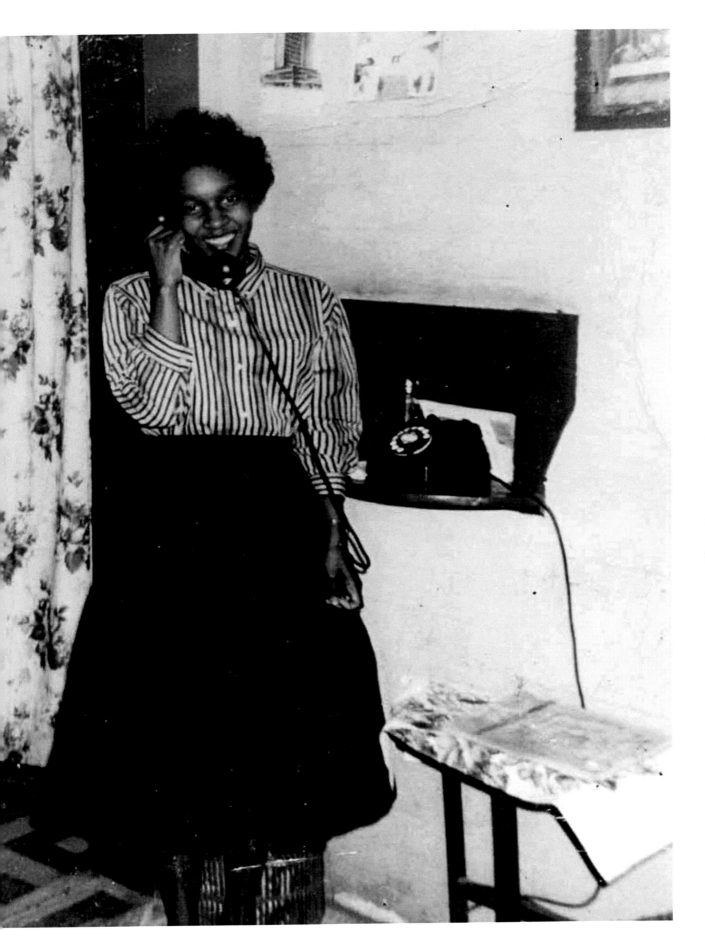

sylvia cartagena
Life-Long Winter Park Resident
september 22 | 2007

These beautifully dressed Orlando-area sixth graders are on a reward trip to the nation's capital. In 1959, the students were chosen for this educational adventure because they demonstrated academic excellence. They boarded the train at Winter Park station for their ride to Washington where, under the watchful encouragement of chaperones, they got to know each other. The talented students pictured here visited all of the capital's national monuments and the White House. We note with pride that many of these participants represented our very own Hannibal Elementary.

1948

Two Hearts That Beat
as one,

I was born in Ocala, Florida on November the 18th, 1922. We moved to Winter Park in 1925. Swoope Avenue – we lived in one of the lumber homes on the other side of the railroad track on the west side of Winter Park, Florida. We lived on Swoope Avenue, Lyman Avenue, Comstock, [and] Pennsylvania Avenue. I moved around. . . [until] we finally got the house on Lyman Avenue right across from the church there. In my early life, I attended Winter Park Elementary School, and I attended Hungerford High School. They used to call me Jimmie Dykes when I was playing ball -- played baseball. I pitched a no hitter in Orlando in 1938. I played for the Winter Park Blue Socks.

I went in the service in 1943 and was in the South Pacific in the Mariana Islands. I got discharged and came back to Philadelphia in 1945. I wanted to learn a trade. I went to night school to be a printer, a photographer, etc. I went to St. Joe University. This was 1948. I was a follower of Paul Robeson. Paul Robeson was speaking at this church – St. Augustine's Presbyterian Church in Philadelphia. I met my wife there. How I met her was [through] my sister. After I met my wife, I didn't see her any more for some time and she met a girl that knew my sister, and she asked the young lady where was the young man Jesse Dykes. [So you could say] I met her through Paul Robeson.

I have family all around here. I come back for vacations, things like that. I left Winter Park in 1939... [but] I kept strong connections.

Jesse Dykes
Long-Time Winter Park Residents
september 22 | 2007

This 1947 photograph features a dapper seated gentleman, Grant Dowdell Sr., in front of his home at 889 W. Comstock Avenue. His namesake son Grant Jr. proudly stands behind him.

As Paulette Perkins explains, "My Granddad was a flagman for the railroad, and he worked there until he retired. His post was at Fairbanks Avenue at the railroad crossing. When it was time for the trains to come, he would come out of the railroad shed and pull the STOP sign and flags out and stop the cars until the trains passed by."

Grant Dowdell Sr. was a founding member of New Hope Baptist Church and his name appears on the 1935 cornerstone. Grant and "Genny" Dowdell parented 18 children, 15 of whom grew to adulthood. Above and beyond their child-rearing responsibilities, Grant's railroad job, and their mutual church associations, each was considered a pillar of the Hannibal Square community.

Rita Allen
Mary Daniel
Longtime Winter Park Residents
october 3 | 2009

Mrs. Viola Lemon Hernandez Hazel, was a descendant of William and Katherine Frazier, who moved to Winter Park in 1875 from Richmond, Virginia. In her writings from the 1960s, she states, "I was born in 1897, in one of the oldest houses in Winter Park, it is called The Horton House. It was a two story building on Carolina Avenue, built in the 1800s and is still there."

Mr. Johnny Horton and his wife Mary built this house, two bedrooms upstairs, living room, dining room, kitchen and bath downstairs. The Horton family owned a lot of property in the area. Today an Affordable Housing Program home occupies the lot.

katrene dowdell bentley
native of winter park
october 3 | 2009

This photograph is of the laying of the first cornerstone for New Hope Baptist Church in 1935. At that time it was called New Hope Missionary Baptist Church. William Ashton Coursen, Esq. had given each black church in Winter Park $7,500. That contribution permitted this congregation to leave their rented space in the Masonic Hall on the corner of Welbourne Avenue and Rear Street (Hannibal Square East). The new church, now a neighborhood institution, was erected on Capen Avenue.

The women pictured on the left were the Eastern Star Ladies. Reverend Sheffield stands over the cornerstone. Notice the Masons in the fez hats to his right. The first little girl in her white dress is young Katrene. The rest of the girls are part of Katrene's family.

Katrene was educated in Winter Park and, after elementary school she went to Hungerford High School in Eatonville. "I grew up in church. I also went to school. But that was our main thing, going to church."

Built in the late 1800s this was the home of the William A. and Cornelia Dixon family located in the 300 block of New England Avenue. According to the 1930 U.S. Census, the family resided in the home with their children William A. Jr. (Billy), Arthur, Emery E., and Emma W.

Years later the home was owned by Faith Horton, who converted it into four apartments. It was later sold to Lonnie and Claudia Rountree and converted to rooms for rent.

Rita Allen
Mary Daniels
Longtime Winter Park Residents
October 3 | 2009

This is Mt. Moriah Missionary Baptist Church Youth Choir, and it was taken in 1938. The reason I recall that it was 1938 is because I'm not in the choir, but my brothers are. I was at Hungerford that particular year. Rev. I. C. Nimmions is the minister. On Sundays, we went to church for bible class at 9:30 in the morning, and we normally remained all day. We had services at 11:00 a.m. and

church was out about 1:30 or 2:00. In some cases, the family brought dinner. We had dinner, then the kids played for a while, then went to BYPU, and then the evening services. So it was always a full day of services. Before this church was built there was a wooden church on the same site. Mr. Richard Robert Hall, Jr. Native of Winter Park February 16 | 2002

Mr. Larkin Franklin was the chauffer in Winter Park for Mr. Frank Spooner. When Mr. Franklin left his birthplace in Oklahoma, he moved to Chicago and met Mr. Spooner. He was employed as Mr. Spooner's chauffer and came with him to Florida. He continued as Mr. Spooner's chauffer here in Winter Park for many years. The vehicle is a Buick Touring Car, circa 1920. Note the cap, gloves, jacket, and tie. They were standard dress for the chauffer for a man of means. **Augustus Franklin**
Life-Long Winter Park Resident
september 22 | 2007

This photograph was taken in 1940 and is a picture of the Winter Park Social Club taken at a banquet at the Everready Club on South Street in Orlando, Florida. My Aunt Lila was quite a socialite! She would have club meetings and parties at Mr. Barbour's house. Mr. Barbour would let her bring her friends over, and they had a lot of fun there. The fellows were not there. When they wanted to have their big gala things, that's when they invited their husbands and

Winter Park
Social Club
March 14, 1940

boyfriends. This event right here is, I guess, a banquet they would have once a year. They got all dressed up and went to Orlando to this club. This building no longer exists, but the Everready Club still exists.

MRS. Annie Burns,
Retired Kindergarten Teacher
Mr. Joe Burns,
Retired Math Instructor
April 17 | 2002

I moved to Canton Park in 1967. When we were living there it was very nice and everybody got along. It was like a big family. The children in the picture are dressed for Easter Sunday. See the white gloves? Kim and Mona are my daughters. Kim is the oldest and Mona is the baby and Ruby Jean is a close friend. The picture was taken in April 1968; Kim was 5, Mona was 1, and Ruby was about 12 years old. I thought this picture would be interesting since they were putting a new place Hannibal Square Community Land Trust Homes there. It took so long to put it (the housing) there.

Helen Perkins Wheeler
Former Winter Park Resident
January 17 | 2005

This 1961 photograph is an eastern view of New England Avenue in the Hannibal Square business district. Today, Dexter's restaurant is on the right corner and Chez Vincent is on the left corner.

Bottom Right:

- Davis Grocery Market, former homestead of Frank R. Israel, Alderman, 1887-1893
- Deluxe Barber Shop, James Dixon and Alonzo Roberts
- New England Laundromat, Clarence "Tank" Moore
- New England Liquor Store, R. Francis and Gladys Harper and John C. Prevatt, former location of a general store owned by Mr. Israel
- Laughlin Hotel, Paul and Chaney Laughlin

Bottom Left:

- Ethel's Diner, Shedrick "Shack" and Ethel Paul which once housed the sundry shop owned by Arthur "Spate" Straughter from 1920 until his death in 1957. The Straughter family still owns the property.
- The Billiard Hall, Roger C. Brinson, opened in 1932 by Spate Straughter
- Moore's Tea Room, Sirilla Moore
- People's Grocery, R. Francis and Gladys Harper and John C. Prevatt, former location of a beer and wine establishment owned by Bill Moore
- The Laundromat, R. Francis and Gladys Harper and John C. Prevatt, former location of the Dixon Barber Shop

Hannibal Square remains pedestrian friendly. Residents and visitors still love their cars. Liquor distributors are still delivering liquor; just to a different clientele.

Annette Taylor Collins
Native of Winter Park
October 3 | 2009